U.S. HISTORY TIMELINES

New Nation
1784-1812

Laura Pratt

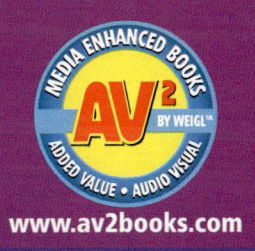

www.av2books.com

MEDIA ENHANCED BOOKS
AV² BY WEIGL
ADDED VALUE • AUDIO VISUAL

AV² provides enriched content that supplements and complements this book. Weigl's AV² books strive to create inspired learning and engage young minds in a total learning experience.

Your AV² Media Enhanced books come alive with...

Audio
Listen to sections of the book read aloud.

Key Words
Study vocabulary, and complete a matching word activity.

Video
Watch informative video clips.

Quizzes
Test your knowledge.

Embedded Weblinks
Gain additional information for research.

Slide Show
View images and captions, and prepare a presentation.

Try This!
Complete activities and hands-on experiments.

... and much, much more!

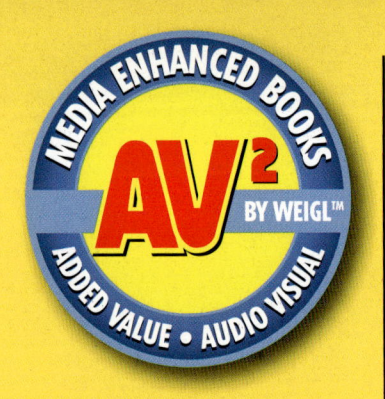

Go to www.av2books.com, and enter this book's unique code.

BOOK CODE

F415520

AV² by Weigl brings you media enhanced books that support active learning.

Published by AV² by Weigl
350 5th Avenue, 59th Floor
New York, NY 10118
Websites: www.av2books.com   www.weigl.com

Copyright ©2015 AV² by Weigl
All rights reserved. No part of this publication may be reproduced, stored in a retrieval system, or transmitted in any form or by any means, electronic, mechanical, photocopying, recording, or otherwise, without the prior written permission of the publisher.

  Library of Congress Control Number: 2014933470
ISBN 978–1–4896–0716–4 (hardcover)
ISBN 978–1–4896–0717–1 (softcover)
ISBN 978–1–4896–0718–8 (single–user eBook)
ISBN 978–1–4896–0719–5 (multi–user eBook)

Printed in the United States of America in North Mankato, Minnesota
1 2 3 4 5 6 7 8 9 0   18 17 16 15 14

052014
WEP301113

Project Coordinator: Aaron Carr
Editor: Pamela Dell
Designer: Mandy Christiansen

Every reasonable effort has been made to trace ownership and to obtain permission to reprint copyright material. The publishers would be pleased to have any errors or omissions brought to their attention so that they may be corrected in subsequent printings.

Weigl acknowledges Getty Images as its primary image supplier for this title.

CONTENTS

- 2 AV² Book Code
- 4 Birth of the Nation
- 6 Setting Up Shop
- 8 Designing a Government
- 10 Convention and Constitution
- 12 George Washington, First U.S. President
- 14 The Government Takes Shape
- 16 Power of the Government
- 18 The Second and Third Presidents
- 20 The Louisiana Purchase
- 22 Stumbling Blocks and Progress
- 24 Shipping Woes
- 26 The War of 1812
- 28 Activity
- 30 Quiz
- 31 Key Words/Index
- 32 Log on to www.av2books.com

September 3, 1783–June 1, 1785

Birth of the Nation

The American colonies had fought a war for independence. The war ended with the signing of the **Treaty** of Paris on September 3, 1783. The treaty included many agreements between the United States and Great Britain. Under this treaty, the United States received new land that stretched west to the Mississippi River.

The United States of America officially became a nation on January 14, 1784. On that day, the U.S. **Congress** accepted the Treaty of Paris. This important agreement formally ended the American Revolutionary War. The new nation had fought Great Britain to free itself from British control. The treaty made this goal a reality.

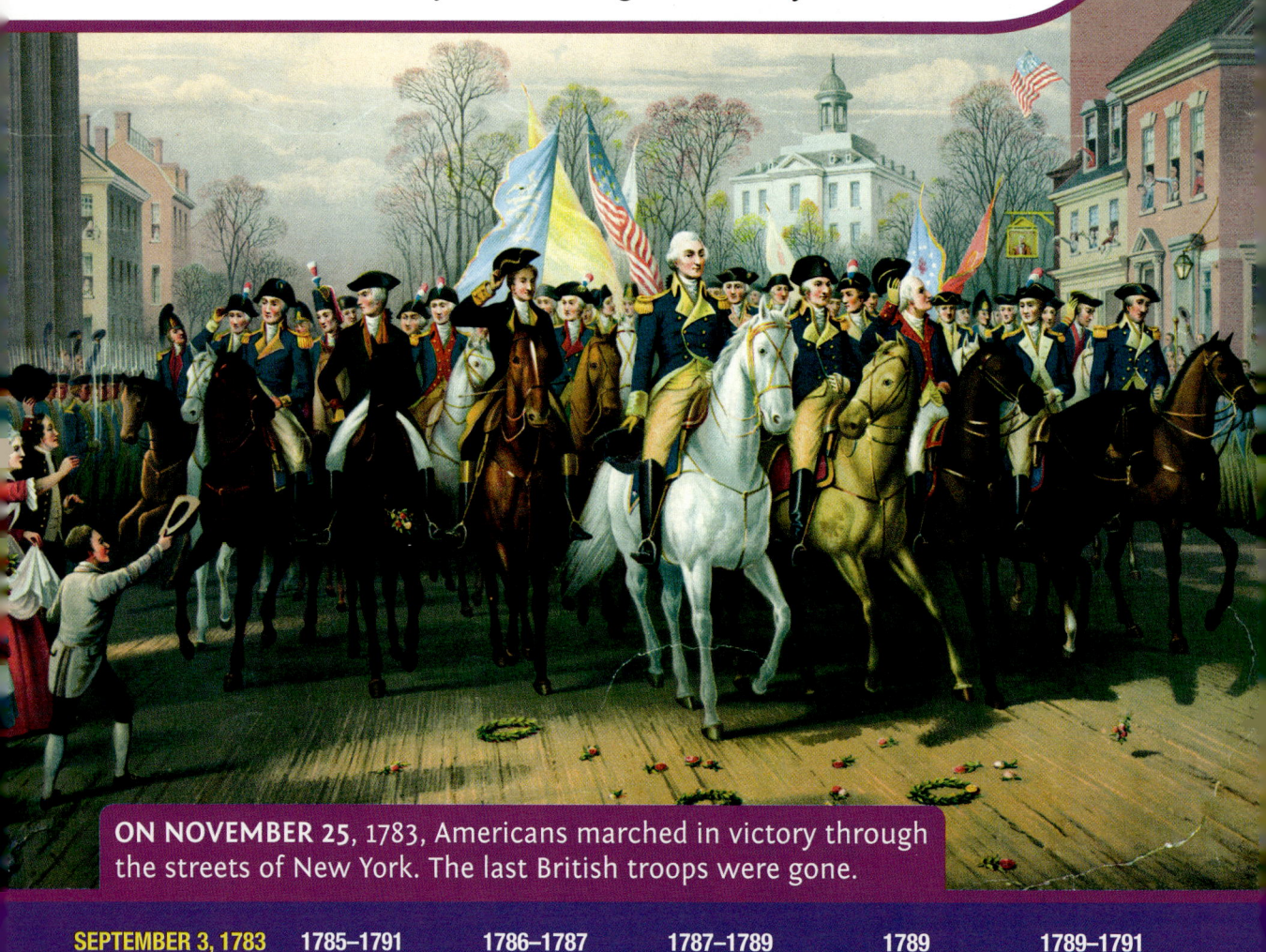

ON NOVEMBER 25, 1783, Americans marched in victory through the streets of New York. The last British troops were gone.

SEPTEMBER 3, 1783 — 1785–1791 — 1786–1787 — 1787–1789 — 1789 — 1789–1791

JUNE 1, 1785

4

SETTLING THE WEST

On April 23, 1784, the U.S. Congress passed the Northwest **Ordinance** of 1784. The ordinance detailed how the United States would divide its western territories into states. It said that the new states would be equal to the 13 original states and always be part of the nation.

TROUBLES WITH THE BRITISH

America's Revolutionary War had broken official ties between the U.S. and Great Britain. On June 1, 1785, however, **Founding Father** John Adams met with King George III in Great Britain. As America's spokesperson, he hoped to smooth relations between the two countries. However, the British government refused to cooperate with Adams.

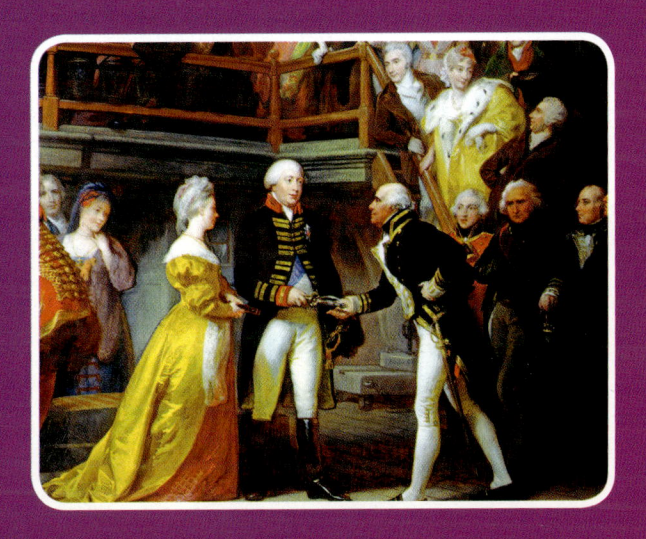

TRADE WITH CHINA

The United States began trading with China in 1784. The Americans sold goods such as furs and special kinds of wood. In return, they took home tea, Chinese silks, cottons, and **tableware**.

1791–1798   1796–1800   1803   1804–1805   1807–1811   1812

5

1785–1791

Setting Up Shop

Since the early 1780s, the United States had operated under the Articles of Confederation. This document served as the nation's first **constitution**. According to the Articles, Congress had no right to tax U.S. citizens. To raise the money it needed, the government decided to sell land. The Land Ordinance of 1785 split the northwest territories into townships. The government then sold these lots to raise money.

The new nation had another money matter to handle. The United States needed a national **currency**. In August 1786, Congress approved a **monetary** system. Two months later, the government set up the United States Mint. The purpose of the mint was to create and issue the nation's money.

TOWNSHIPS CREATED BY the Land Ordinance of 1785 were made up of 36 lots. Each lot was 640 acres (2.6 square kilometers) and cost $640.

1783–1785   1785   1786–1787   1787–1789   1789   1789–1791

6

1791

The first U.S. Mint was in Philadelphia, Pennsylvania. In 1791, the First Bank of the United States was created. The bank's job was to create a standard form of money for the whole country.

1791–1798   1796–1800   1803   1804–1805   1807–1811   1812

7

1786–May 27, 1787

Designing a Government

By 1786, the United States had been united as a nation for 10 years. By that time, it had become clear that the Articles of Confederation were not working. The Articles did not provide enough guidance for running the new nation. Some people believed the **federal** government needed more control in running the country. They thought this would help keep the country united.

To address this matter, political leaders gathered in Philadelphia for the Constitutional Convention. **Delegates** from nearly all the states came to the convention. Their goal was to create a new and better form of federal government. They agreed that the government would have three branches. That way, no single part of the government could become too powerful. These three branches were the legislative, the executive, and the judicial branches.

THE CONSTITUTIONAL CONVENTION began on May 25, 1787. It was not long before George Washington was elected president of the convention.

1783–1785   1785–1791   1786   1787–1789   1789   1789–1791

MAY 25, 1787

"The people are the [rulers] of this country . . . "
John Jay, first Supreme Court chief justice

THE THREE BRANCHES OF THE UNITED STATES GOVERNMENT

EXECUTIVE BRANCH
The president is the head of the executive branch. The executive branch oversees the highest level of government. The president has the power to sign laws into being or to **veto** them. The vice president and members of the **cabinet** also belong to this branch.

LEGISLATIVE BRANCH
The legislative branch includes the Senate and the House of Representatives. Together, the senators and representatives make up the U.S. Congress. The most important duty of the legislative branch is making laws.

JUDICIAL BRANCH
The judicial branch is the U.S. court system. It is made up of three levels of courts. These are the district courts, the courts of appeals, and the supreme court. The Supreme Court is the highest court in the nation.

SINCE 1869, THE U.S. Supreme Court has included eight associate justices, or judges, and one chief justice. They meet at the Supreme Court Building in Washington, D.C.

1791–1798   1796–1800   1803   1804–1805   1807–1811   1812

1787–March 4, 1789

Convention and Constitution

Before the Constitutional Convention, the young American nation had been suffering growing pains. Citizens were in disagreement over many issues. The government was unable to pay back its loans. The country could not collect the money it needed to operate. Other nations saw the United States as unimportant.

The convention delegates realized the United States needed to become stronger and more stable. To do that, it would need a more powerful federal government. A new constitution would help make the roles of government clearer. The new constitution would also outline how the government would be run.

The final draft of the constitution was ready in only a few months. On September 17, 1787, the convention ended. Now it was time to take that document to the states for their approval.

CONVENTION DELEGATES INCLUDED farmers, bankers, and businessmen. Others were educators or Revolutionary War veterans.

1783–1785 | 1785–1791 | 1786–1787 | **1787** | 1789 | 1789–1791

MARCH 4, 1789

EIGHT MEN AT the Constitutional Convention were also signers of the U.S. Declaration of Independence in 1776. One was Benjamin Franklin. At 81, he was the oldest delegate at the convention.

JAMES MADISON WAS a convention delegate from Virginia. He later came to be known as the "Father of the Constitution" because of his important role in creating that document.

The U.S. Constitution

After the Constitutional Convention, the states had to vote to decide if they would accept the new constitution. In June 1788, New Hampshire became the ninth state to accept the constitution. This was enough votes to make the document the highest law of the United States. The new government began on March 4, 1789.

By the Numbers

STATES REPRESENTED:
12 – Rhode Island did not attend

TOTAL NUMBER OF DELEGATES CHOSEN TO ATTEND: 74

NUMBER OF DELEGATES THAT ACTUALLY ATTENDED: 55

NUMBER OF DELEGATES THAT SIGNED THE CONSTITUTION: 39

1791–1798   1796–1800   1803   1804–1805   1807–1811   1812

February 4–April 1789

George Washington, First U.S. President

The first United States election was held on February 4, 1789. That day, 69 members of **Electoral College** voted on who would be the country's president. Each man filled in a **ballot**. Then the ballots had to be counted. In April 1789, the election results were announced. George Washington was the **unanimous** winner.

Washington had led the Continental Army in the Revolutionary War. He was a delegate to the **Second Continental Congress** and president of the Continental Convention. These roles earned him great trust and respect. John Adams was elected vice president.

AT 57, WASHINGTON felt too old to govern a nation. He accepted the job out of his strong sense of duty.

1783–1785　1785–1791　1786–1787　1787–1789　**FEBRUARY 4, 1789**　1789–1791

APRIL 1789

George Washington served two terms as president. His presidency lasted until March 4, 1797. He is remembered for shaping the government and the role of president. Washington's decisions about this role and its powers guided future presidents. Washington died on December 14, 1799. In his will, he granted freedom to his slaves.

1791–1798 1796–1800 1803 1804–1805 1807–1811 1812

1789–March 1, 1791

The Government Takes Shape

Congress worked through the summer of 1789 to shape the new government. It organized many new departments. Some of these included the Department of Foreign Affairs, the War Department, and the **Treasury**. Congress also set up the country's judicial system, including the Supreme Court.

The constitution was barely official before people began calling for changes, however. In September 1789, Congress proposed 12 constitutional **amendments**. In 1791, delegates from each state approved the first 10 of these amendments. These 10 points defined citizens' rights in various areas. Together, these 10 amendments are known as the Bill of Rights.

THE U.S. CONSTITUTION begins by stating that the people of country have good reasons for creating a constitution. Two of these reasons are to form a stronger nation and ensure freedom.

1783–1785 1785–1791 1786–1787 1787–1789 1789 1789

MARCH 1, 1791

On March 1, 1790, Congress passed the **Census** Act. The first census showed that fewer than 4 million people then lived in the United States. However, this count only included the first 13 states, the Southwest Territory, and the districts of Maine, Vermont, and Kentucky. Great Britain's population was nearly 15 million. France had 26 million. In the United States, only Philadelphia, New York, and three other cities had more than 10,000 residents.

1ST AMENDMENT
This amendment describes the rights Americans consider most important. These are the freedom of religion, freedom of speech, and freedom of the press.

6TH AMENDMENT
This amendment states that anyone accused of a crime has the right to a public trial. It also ensures that people will be given help in their legal defense.

1791–1798

Power of the Government

As time passed, new states joined the **Union**. Still, the government faced troubles from both citizens and foreign enemies. Taxes were one problem. Americans resisted paying taxes. In 1791, Congress set a tax on whiskey sold in the United States. Some Pennsylvania **whiskey** sellers refused to pay the tax. By 1794, many of them were openly rebelling against the tax.

President Washington wanted to prevent the violent Whiskey Rebellion from spreading to other states. He led 13,000 troops in an early fight against the rebels. The rebellion lasted into the fall. In the end, the government's success proved its power.

In 1798, Congress passed the **Alien** and **Sedition** Acts. These laws gave the government broad powers. However, some of these laws went against the Bill of Rights. Many people were against these laws. Many of the laws were allowed to expire.

TEMPERS FLARED DURING the Whiskey Rebellion. One group of rebels even went after a federal tax collector and burned down his home.

1783–1785   1785–1791   1786–1787   1787–1789   1789   1789–1791

GENERAL DANIEL MORGAN was a highly respected officer who helped put down the Whiskey Rebellion.

The Alien and Sedition Acts

These laws showed how powerful a government might become.

1. The Alien Enemies Act defined how the government would decide if someone from an enemy nation was a threat to the nation during wartime.

2. The Alien Friends Act gave the president power to **deport** foreigners during peacetime.

3. The Naturalization Act made it harder for foreigners to become citizens.

4. The Sedition Act made it illegal for any citizen or group to go against anything the government chose to do. Writing, speaking, or printing anything negative against the president was also illegal. Of all the acts, people found this one the most alarming.

1796–1800

The Second and Third Presidents

Federalist John Adams was elected president in 1796. He was the nation's second president. Adams only served one term. His dealings with other countries made him unpopular with the public.

In 1800, the U.S. capital moved from Philadelphia to Washington, D.C. The Federalists wanted a strong central government. Thomas Jefferson belonged to the Democratic Republican Party. This party believed the states should have more power. The Federalists and the Republicans disagreed on many other issues as well.

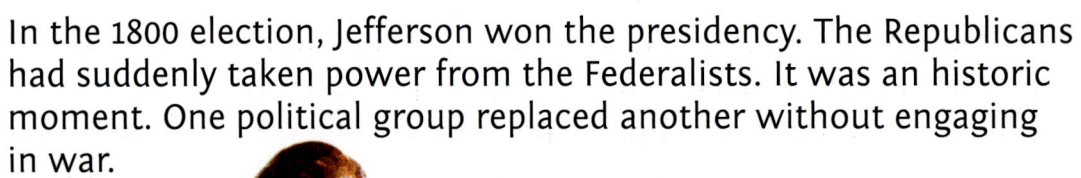

In the 1800 election, Jefferson won the presidency. The Republicans had suddenly taken power from the Federalists. It was an historic moment. One political group replaced another without engaging in war.

IN 1776, THOMAS Jefferson was the main author of the Declaration of Independence. Adams was also one of its creators. Both men died on July 4, 1826. This was the 50th anniversary of the signing of the Declaration.

1783–1785   1785–1791   1786–1787   1787–1789   1789   1789–1791

As president, Thomas Jefferson sought to show his connection to the common people. His forward-thinking views on individual freedom, religion, and education still have power today. Jefferson believed in the strict separation of church and state. He did not want the government interfering in citizens' religious activities. Although he was a slaveholder, Jefferson was in favor of freedom for the enslaved.

THE SON OF John Adams, John Quincy Adams became the nation's sixth president. Only one other father and son have both been president. They were 41st president George H. W. Bush and 43rd president George W. Bush.

1791–1798 1796 1803 1804–1805 1807–1811 1812

1800

May 2, 1803

The Louisiana Purchase

Early Americans had a strong drive to expand U.S. territory to the west. In 1803, the government, under President Jefferson, bought land from the French. In the deal, the United States agreed to pay $15 million for New Orleans, Louisiana, and a great deal of land stretching all the way to the Canadian border in the north.

The Louisiana Purchase was the largest land purchase in the new country's history. This newly added territory stretched more than 828,000 square miles (2,144,520 sq. km). It included Louisiana and all or part of what later became 14 different states. With this purchase, the size of U.S.–owned territory almost doubled.

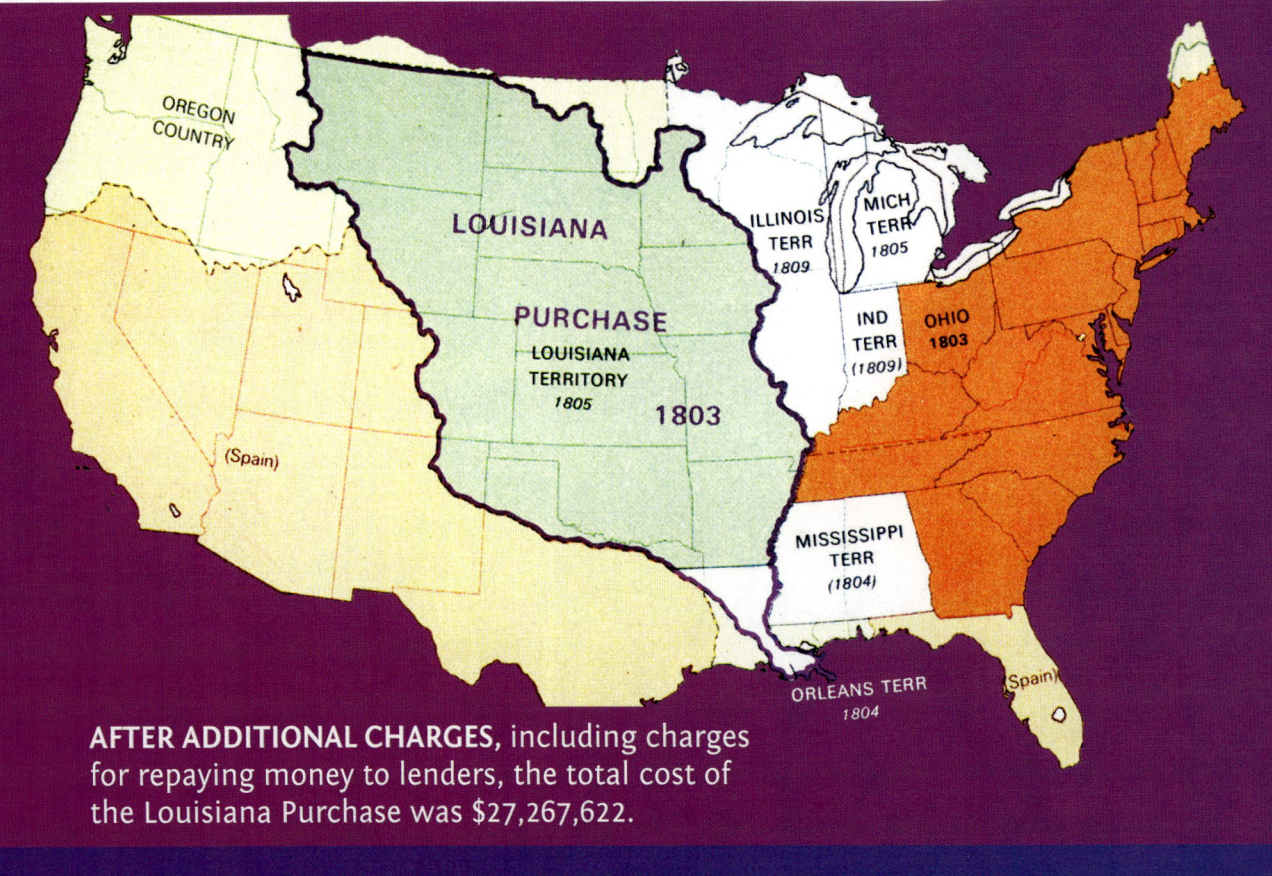

AFTER ADDITIONAL CHARGES, including charges for repaying money to lenders, the total cost of the Louisiana Purchase was $27,267,622.

After finalizing the Louisiana Purchase, President Jefferson sent explorers Meriwether Lewis and William Clark on an expedition through the new lands. Lewis and Clark were guided by a young Shoshone American Indian woman named Sacajawea.

THE FRENCH CONNECTION

Louisiana was named after King Louis XIV, who ruled France from 1643 to 1714. At the time of the Louisiana Purchase, French, Spanish, African, and Caribbean peoples lived together in and around New Orleans. This area was a "melting pot" of people. They lived mostly in peace and often intermarried. The descendants of these people came to be called Creoles.

The term "Creole" has a long history. After the Louisiana Purchase, people of French and Spanish descent began calling themselves Creoles. This was to separate themselves from the Americans of English descent who had taken over the land. Today, the term "Creole" has many different meanings. It is applied not only to people but also to music, food, and spoken language.

| 1791–1798 | 1796–1800 | MAY 2, 1803 | 1804–1805 | 1807–1811 | 1812 |

21

June 1804–1805

Stumbling Blocks and Progress

In the early 1800s, Thomas Jefferson was nearing the end of his first presidential term. The United States was still defining itself. The government was still testing the limits of its power.

In these early years, national focus moved between events going on both near and far. The Lewis and Clark Expedition began in 1804, starting out on the Missouri River. Other events included the death of an important politician, wars abroad, and new constitutional amendments.

1804

In the earliest U.S. presidential elections, the Electoral College voted only for a presidential candidate. Whoever came in second automatically became vice president. Signed in June 1804, the 12th Amendment to the Constitution changed this. It called for presidential electors to vote for both a president and a vice president. This law went into effect for the first time in the 1804 election.

| 1783–1785 | 1785–1791 | 1786–1787 | 1787–1789 | 1789 | 1789–1791 |

1804

In 1804, Founding Father Alexander Hamilton was the leader of the Federalist Party. He had supported Thomas Jefferson in the 1800 election. New York senator Aaron Burr did not like this. He had hoped to win the presidency himself. Angered by many of Hamilton's political moves, Burr challenged his enemy to a duel. At the July 11 duel, Burr fired the fatal shot. Hamilton died the next day. The public outcry was so great that it ended Burr's political career.

1804

In the presidential election of 1804 President Thomas Jefferson ran against Federalist Charles Pinckney. Jefferson easily defeated Pinckney. His margin of victory was 45.6 percent. This number remains the highest in a presidential election involving multiple candidates from major parties. New Yorker George Clinton won the vice presidency.

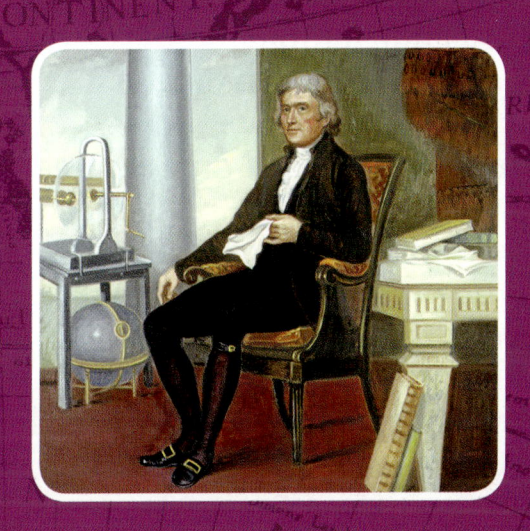

1805

At the beginning of the 1800s, the United States battled for the first time overseas. In what is known as the First Barbary War, U.S. warships fought against the Barbary pirates of North Africa. The four-year war ended in 1805.

1791–1798 | 1796–1800 | 1803 | **JUNE 1804** | 1807–1811 | 1812

1805

23

1807–1811

Shipping Woes

In 1807, Great Britain was at war with France. For the United States, trade with either country was now nearly impossible. After the British navy captured American merchant ships, Congress took action. In December 1807, the government passed the Embargo Act. This law put a stop to all **export** shipping. It also limited **imports** of British goods into the United States.

Jefferson had hoped the Embargo Act would force the British to leave American ships alone. Instead, it brought years of hardship and poverty for the American people. In 1809, the president signed the Non-Intercourse Act. This opened up U.S. trade with nations other than France and Great Britain.

Toward Ending Slavery

In 1808, the Act Prohibiting Importation of Slaves took effect on January 1. This federal law made it illegal to import slaves into any U.S.-held territory. Despite this, the slaves continued to be imported and traded in the United States until after the American Civil War.

In the early 1800s, Congress did not want to upset slaveholders. Yet before 1808, it made some small moves toward ending slavery. The Slave Trade Act of 1794 made it unlawful to make, load, outfit, equip, or send to sea any ship used for slave trading. In 1798, a new law called for a penalty of $300 per slave for anyone convicted of illegally importing slaves.

ANYONE CAUGHT VIOLATING the Slave Trade Act paid dearly. The fee for building or owning a ship made to hold slaves was $20,000.

1791–1798 1796–1800 1803 1804–1805 1807 1812

1811

1812

The War of 1812

The United States had fought Great Britain once before. The Revolutionary War had brought freedom from British rule, but it did not end the issues between the two countries. Great Britain was interfering in American shipping and trade. The United States also hoped to push the British out of Canada and expand its boundaries north.

These issues led to the War of 1812. In the end, neither side clearly won. The war formally ended with the Treaty of Ghent. This treaty, was signed in Ghent, Belgium. Under the terms of the treaty, Canada would stay under British control, but Great Britain would stop interfering with the United States. For the United States, expansion to the west was the next order of business.

DURING THE WAR of 1812, Americans fought the British, their American Indian allies, and Canadian colonists. For 32 months, battles raged on U.S. and Canadian soil as well as at sea.

1783–1785   1785–1791   1786–1787   1787–1789   1789   1789–1791

News traveled slowly in 1815. The Treaty of Ghent was signed on December 24, 1814. Not aware of the agreement to end the war, some forces were still fighting. General Andrew Jackson's troops defeated the British at the Battle of New Orleans on January 8, 1815. On February 17, President Madison formally declared an end to the war.

| 1791–1798 | 1796–1800 | 1803 | 1804–1805 | 1807–1811 | 1812 |

Activity

Create a Concept Web

Timelines are only a beginning. They provide an overview of the key events and important people that shaped history. Now, research in the library and on the internet to discover the rest of the story of how the United States grew as a nation.

Use a concept web to organize your ideas. Use the questions in the concept web to guide your research. When finished, use the completed web to help you write your report.

BENJAMIN FRANKLIN WAS the only Founding Father to sign all four documents that officially established the United States as a new nation.

Concept Web

Important Events
- What significant events shaped the times or the person you're writing about?
- Were there any major events that triggered some turning point in the life or the time you are writing about?

Key People
- Discuss one or two main figures who had an impact on the times, event, or person you are researching.
- What negative or positive actions by people had a lasting effect on history?

Historic Places
- Discuss some of the most important places related to the subject of your research.
- Are there some important places that are not well-known today?
- If so, what are they, and why were they important at the time or to your subject?

Causes
- How was your subject affected by important historical moments of the time?
- Was there any chain of events to cause a particular outcome in the event, time, or the life you are researching?

Write a History Report

Obstacles
- What were some of the most difficult moments or events in the life of the person or in the historical timeline of the topic you are researching?
- Were there any particular people who greatly aided in the overcoming of obstacles?

Outcome and Lasting Effects
- What was the outcome of this chain of events?
- Was there a lasting effect on your subject?
- What is the importance of these "stepping stones" of history? How might the outcome have changed if things had happened differently?

Into the Future
- What lasting impact did your subject have on history?
- Is that person, time, or event well-known today?
- Have people's attitudes changed from back then until now about your subject?
- Do people think differently today about the subject than they did at the time the event happened or the person was alive?

Quiz

1. Which U.S. president was elected unanimously?

2. What agreement ended the War of 1812?

3. Who was the second president of the United States?

4. What U.S. law made the use of slave ships illegal?

5. How many constitutional amendments does the Bill of Rights include?

6. What political party did Thomas Jefferson belong to?

7. What city did the U.S. capital move to in 1800?

8. How much did the Louisiana Purchase cost the United States?

9. Who did Aaron Burr kill in an 1804 duel?

10. Who had the nickname "the Father of the Constitution"?

11. Who was Lewis and Clark's Indian guide?

12. What two countries were involved in the War of 1812?

ANSWERS
1. George Washington
2. The Treaty of Ghent
3. John Adams
4. The Slave Trade Act of 1794
5. 10
6. The Democratic Republican Party
7. Washington, D.C.
8. $15 million
9. Alexander Hamilton
10. James Madison
11. Sacajawea
12. Great Britain and the United States

Key Words

alien: a person from another country

amendments: additions or changes to something that already exists

ballot: a vote in an election

cabinet: people who head the main government departments

census: official population count

Congress: the main lawmaking body of the United States

constitution: a document that outlines how a country's government will be set up and what its powers will be

currency: money

delegates: people selected to act in the name of a larger group

deport: force to leave the country

Electoral College: a group of representatives from each state who vote to elect the president and vice president

export: goods shipped out of a country

federal: the national level of government

Federalist: a supporter of a strong federal government; part of the Federalist Party

Founding Father: one of the men who set up the U.S. government

imports: goods brought into a country

monetary: having to do with money

ordinance: an official order

Second Continental Congress: the group of states' representatives who together ran the government from 1775 to 1781

sedition: acting or speaking in a way that encourages people to rebel against authority

tableware: dishes, eating utensils, and glasses used to eat meals

Treasury: the branch of government in charge of handling money

treaty: a formal written agreement

unanimous: all in agreement

Union: another name for the United States, used mostly before and during the Civil War

veto: to reject, or overturn, a decision made by a governing body

whiskey: an alcoholic drink made from grains

Index

Adams, John 5, 12, 18, 19, 30
Alien and Sedition Act 16, 17

Bill of Rights 14, 16, 30
branches of government 8, 9

Census Act 15
Constitutional Convention 8, 10, 11

Democratic Republican Party 18, 30

Embargo Act 24

Federalist Party 18, 23
First Amendment 15
Franklin, Benjamin 11, 28

George III, King 5

Hamilton, Alexander 23, 30

Jefferson, Thomas 5, 18, 19, 20, 21, 22, 23, 24, 30

Land Ordinance of 1785 6
Lewis and Clark Expedition 21, 22, 30
Louisiana Purchase 20, 21, 30
Louis XIV, King 21

Madison, James 11, 24, 27, 30

Ordinance of 1784 5

Second Amendment 15
Slave Trade Act 25, 30

Treaty of Ghent 26, 27, 30
Treaty of Paris 4, 26
Twelfth Amendment 22

War of 1812 24, 26, 27, 30
Washington, George 8, 12, 13, 16, 18, 30
Whiskey Rebellion 16, 17

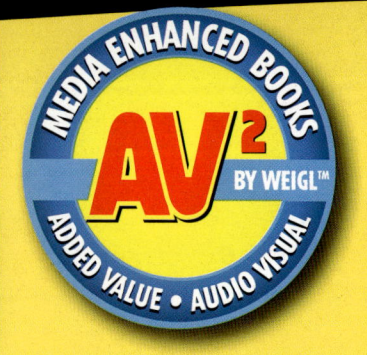

Log on to www.av2books.com

AV² by Weigl brings you media enhanced books that support active learning. Go to www.av2books.com, and enter the special code found on page 2 of this book. You will gain access to enriched and enhanced content that supplements and complements this book. Content includes video, audio, weblinks, quizzes, a slide show, and activities.

AV² Online Navigation

Audio
Listen to sections of the book read aloud.

Book Pages
AV² pages directly correspond to pages in the book.

Video
Watch informative video clips.

Key Words
Study vocabulary, and complete a matching word activity.

Embedded Weblinks
Gain additional information for research.

Quizzes
Test your knowledge.

Slide Show
View images and captions, and prepare a presentation.

Try This!
Complete activities and hands-on experiments.

AV² was built to bridge the gap between print and digital. We encourage you to tell us what you like and what you want to see in the future.

Sign up to be an AV² Ambassador at www.av2books.com/ambassador.

Due to the dynamic nature of the Internet, some of the URLs and activities provided as part of AV² by Weigl may have changed or ceased to exist. AV² by Weigl accepts no responsibility for any such changes. All media enhanced books are regularly monitored to update addresses and sites in a timely manner. Contact AV² by Weigl at 1-866-649-3445 or av2books@weigl.com with any questions, comments, or feedback.